Chakras

You May Achieve Higher Consciousness And Spiritual Healing By Opening Your Third Eye Chakra

(The Chakras: Investigating The Energy Centre Of The Body To Achieve Spiritual Harmony)

Alasdair Nuttall

TABLE OF CONTENT

Your Solar Plexus And Your Personal Endeavors 1

Problems With The Kidneys And The Liver 9

Light Therapy For The Healing Of The Chakras 17

What Can Obstruct A Chakra? 22

A Color Therapy Approach To Restoring Chakra Balance 42

The Exchange Of Chakra Energies Between Two Different People 59

The Phrase "Manipura" The Solar Plexus Chakra, Often Known As The Sun Energy Center 65

The Significance Of The Chakras 77

Methods Of Breathing That Will Assist You In Keeping Your Chakras Open 80

How The Seven Chakras Affect Our Everyday Lives 99

The Seven Chakras 113

This Is The Throat Chakra. 128

Symptoms Of A Disrupted Energy Balance In The Heart Chakra 135

Symptoms And Indications Of An Unbalanced Sacral Chakra.. 140

The Chakra At The Crown..................................... 146

Acquiring A Wise Perspective............................. 152

The Chakra Of Love Located In The Heart..... 158

Obstacles Presented By The Chakras 171

Your Solar Plexus And Your Personal Endeavors

The energy that is provided by our Solar Plexus is the energy that assists us in discovering and achieving success. It instills in us the resilient mentalities necessary to push through adversity without showing fear. It inspires us to attack challenges with the self-assurance and audacity that ultimately contribute to our achievements. However, there are instances when we have difficulty channeling the energy of the Solar Plexus, which may result in feelings of poor self-esteem or a lack of confidence. When we are missing these essential components of success, the obstacles we face suddenly become more difficult, and it may seem that it will be impossible for us to achieve any level of achievement. We are fortunate in that the capacity to channel the energy of the Solar Plexus helps enhance our confidence and raises our self-esteem, which provides us with the resources necessary to complete our own pursuits and find success in them. Therefore, if you feel that your self-esteem, confidence, or sense of self-worth are diminishing slowly or fast at a time when you need them the most, do the following exercise:

Breathing That Empowers You

1. Make a quick mental note of the feelings you experience in your stomach and/or chest as you inhale and exhale just before you are presented with a tough or nerve-wracking scenario, or at the time that you are confronted with the event itself. 2. Do you exhale with an air of bravery and self-assurance? Or do you feel even the tiniest tremor?

2. Take note, if appropriate, of your hands trembling, the erratic rise and fall

of your chest as you breathe, or the uneasy feelings that appear to dominate your stomach.

3. Once you have finished the preceding evaluations, the next step is to get control of your breathing. Your body will obey your instruction to gently inhale and exhale if you tell it to. Your order will be followed by the naturally automatic action of breathing that your body does.

4. Keep in mind that I am in charge of my body. I am in charge of my circumstances. I am able to take charge. I am the one in charge here.

5. Make sure you keep your breathing under control until all of the unsteadiness, shivering, and anxiousness leaves your body. You should have the sense that you are in command of the situation and be able to face the challenge with the same level of audacity

and self-assurance that you had before, or perhaps more so.

The opening of the Chakra of the Root...

Tiger's Eye, Bloodstone, Black Obsidian, Hematite, Garnet, Ruby, Jasper, Red Jasper, and Smokey Quartz are all examples of crystals.

Nutmeg, cinnamon, ginger, cypress, and sandalwood are some of the herbs and oils that are used.

Thunder, bij mantra: Lam, and the note C at a frequency of 256 Hz

Protein, root vegetables, minerals, foods that grow deep in the ground, and red foods like apples, raspberries, tomatoes, strawberries, cherries, pomegranate, radish, beets, and watermelon are examples of foods that include these nutrients.

Tadasana, Uttanasana, Virabhadrasana, and Balasana are all examples of yoga poses.

Bones, blood, the immune system, the colon, the rectum, feet and legs, and scent are all governed by this organ. Structure, community and tribe, survival instincts, family, organizations, safety, and security; a feeling of belonging; the capacity to be anchored; sense of safety and security;

"At every moment, I am blessed with divine assistance."

The Root chakra is the starting point for any spiritual work. Feeling at home on Earth is something that may be facilitated by the Root chakra. It is your link and support system inside the Earth community as well as the Earth itself. If you have a blocked Root chakra, you will not feel as if you belong in this world. It's possible that you feel like you're at odds with yourself, your profession, or your family. You have the ability to release this energy to assist you in regaining your equilibrium.

It is necessary to have a strong connection with the earth in order to activate the Root chakra. Spend some time outdoors in the fresh air and stroll barefoot across the grass. One thing you can do anyplace to feel the energy flowing through the Root chakra is to get up and pound your feet quickly on the ground. This will activate the chakra. Chanting the bij mantra Lam is my personal favorite thing to do in order to open the Root chakra. If you feel unsteady for whatever reason, doing this action will instantly assist you in vibrating at a higher frequency. Imagine that a brilliant crimson light is emanating from the base of your spine while you do this mantra. You have a responsibility to look after your physical health. You also need to work on improving your health. Eat a diet higher in protein! Even vegans and vegetarians have to make sure they receive enough protein in their diet. Because sleep may help you feel more rooted in reality, you should prioritize getting enough of it. I find that a sound at 256 Hz puts me to sleep quickly and easily. This chakra responds extremely well to aromatherapy and yoga as a form of treatment. Which aromas make you feel the most protected?

Your sense of stability and grounding will improve as a result of your work on the Root chakra. When your Root chakra is blocked, it is the equivalent of when the wheels of your automobile are loose. It is essential that you feel safe and secure, which is why the Root chakra is of the utmost significance. The process of unlocking your Root chakra is one that never comes to a conclusion. It is not something you uncover just once and then forget about. Amazing progress may be made with even a little amount of effort put in each day.

Problems With The Kidneys And The Liver

First Position The hands of the healer should be placed in a parallel position from the area of the upper teeth to the forehead, in the same position to the right and left of the nose. This is the first posture.

In the second position, the ridges of the pelvic bones should be pressed between the balls of the thumbs. To produce a V shape at the pubic bone, the fingertips of both hands should be brought in close proximity to one another.

Placed in Third Position

Put your hands on your lower ribs, just over your kidney, and relax.

Place in Order Four

Put one hand on the sacrum plate, and the other hand, while applying little pressure, should be placed vertically below it.

Fifth Position Wrap your hands around your ankles in this position.

Problems with the Liver

The Leading Position

A hand should be put on the right side of the lowest ribs, and another hand should be positioned below the first hand.

Second Position Raise one hand so that it is directly over the navel. Maintain the position of your other hand below it.

Third Position Bring the palms of the hands together and place them on top of the shoulder blades.

Fractures, Arthritis, and Other Ailments

Symptoms of arthritis

The Leading Position

It is important for the healer to place their hands on the patient's lower ribs, just above the kidney.

The hands should then be placed on the bottoms of the feet, which is the second position. More specifically, the tips of the big toes need to be protected by the covering.

Pain

The Leading Position

Put your hands in this space between your shoulder blades and your shoulders.

Second Position At this point, move your hands such that they are resting on top of your shoulder blades. If the patient is complaining of discomfort in their bones, you should place one hand above and one hand below the major cervical vertebra at the nape of the neck.

If there is a discomfort in the hips and legs, you should channel the universal energy to the whole back and outside of the hips.

The postures below may be used to administer Reiki to the top of the shoulder in order to alleviate discomfort in the arm.

The first position for the hands involves positioning them between the shoulders and the blades of the shoulders.

The second position requires that the hands remain on the blades of the shoulder.

A number of fractures

After the bones have been aligned using the hand positions that are detailed below, regular Reiki therapy is required to be carried out.

First Position The practitioner should put one hand in a position that is parallel to the right and left side of the nose from the area of the upper teeth down to the forehead of the patient.

A hand should be put lightly on the lowest ribs, and another hand should be placed just below it. This is the second position.

Placed in Third Position

One hand should be put on the sacrum plate, and the other hand should be positioned vertically below while applying a little bit of additional pressure.

The fourth position calls for the healer to lay their hands on the bottoms of the patient's feet, encircling the big toes and covering them from the tips down.

Diabetes, Asthma, and Heart Attack
Diabetes, Asthma, and Heart Attack

If you have diabetes and are receiving Reiki therapy, you should focus a lot of attention on your elbows and give them the postures below.

The Leading Position

It is important for the healer to arrange their hands so that they are parallel to the right and left sides of the patient's nose and reach from the top of the head to the area of the upper teeth.

The hands should be positioned on the left side of the lower ribs and below them in the second position.

Placed in Third Position

The practitioner of healing should make the letter "T" with their hands by placing one hand over the thymus and the other hand at a straight angle below and between the breasts.

In the fourth position, the hands are positioned so that they are resting on the soles of the feet, and the big toes are covered starting from their tips.

Symptoms of asthma

The Leading Position

The hands of the healer should cup the recipient's head behind the ears, and the healer's fingers should be placed on the medulla oblongata.

Second Position In the second position, the practitioner should put their hands in a parallel posture to the right and left of the nose. This should be done beginning at the forehead and continuing all the way down to the area around the upper teeth.

Placed in Third Position

One hand should be put over the thymus, and the other hand should be positioned at a right angle between the breasts in order to make the letter T.

Fourth Position In this position, the thumb balls are placed on the ridges of the pelvic bone, and the tips of the hands are brought in close to each other at the pubic bone, making the letter V.

Light Therapy For The Healing Of The Chakras

The Light and the Chakras

Working with light and visualizing a brighter future are both essential components of chakra balance. You may do this by just picturing the light entering various chakras in your body as a type of meditation, or you can utilize real color therapy, such as lamps of varying colors or clothing of varying colors, to surround yourself with the energy needed to accomplish this.

The chakras have a favorable reaction to color therapy because, of all the methods of chakra balancing, colors are the ones that are closest to pure energy. This explains why color therapy works so effectively. The light that originates from natural sources, such as the sun, moon, and stars, is universally acknowledged to be of the highest quality. We have to make sure that we spend a lot of time in front of this light source if we want to seem as natural as possible. Because we are creatures composed of energy in its most dense and tangible form, we have the ability to return ourselves to a more refined frequency by using the colors of the spectrum to bring our chakras into alignment.

If you choose to surround yourself with or mentally promote specific colors, you will actually be 'feeding' or protecting that chakra. This is because each chakra has its own color linked with it, and you will see that hue when you look at each chakra.

Utilizing Color Therapy in a Variety of Ways

Put on the color that has been selected for your outerwear.

Put on some clothing of the selected hue or tie a scarf of that color around the chakra of your choice.

While you are lying down, place a light scarf or another light material of the color of your choice over the chakra, meditate, and allow yourself to relax.

Imagine that the color you've picked is completely surrounding you and enveloping you.

Carry along with you a crystal that is tinted in the color of your choice, and at some point throughout the day, position it in front of you and face it in your direction. Imagine that it is radiating that hue directly into the sensitive body you have!

The Various Colors That Represent the Chakras

Diamond of white color - This is a nearly dazzling, cleansing light that energizes you and lifts your energy level to higher spiritual realms. It is used for the crown chakra, which is located at the top of the head.

The emerald green flame is a kind of therapeutic viridian light that is physiologically nourishing and utilized to cure the heart chakra as well as lower chakras.

The violet flame is connected to the sacral chakra as well as the chakras in the body that are located below the neck. It symbolizes the union of the divine male and the divine feminine in order to heal your feelings and your heart.

The rose pink light, which is most closely related with the sacrum and the root chakras, imbues your aura with an unwavering sense of safety and protection. Because of this, it is an ideal light for the healing of the inner child.

Yellow, also known as sunshine yellow, is connected to our sacral, solar plexus, and heart chakras. This color is symbolic of Christ awareness as well as kindness, benevolence, and giving.

Gold light is a more stronger form of the sunny yellow beam; this hue is related instead with the full body as well as each chakra, and it is beneficial for producing serenity, eliminating tension, and establishing harmony. After putting in a lot of effort, this is a great way to wind down.

What Can Obstruct A Chakra?

Since you now have a better understanding of what chakras are, you may be curious in the factors that might lead to a blockage in your chakras and, therefore, an impairment in their ability to perform their intended functions. If one or more of your chakras are blocked, you may experience feelings of illness or unhealthiness on both the physical and emotional levels, as well as a general sense of exhaustion.

People who have chakras that are blocked often report feeling as if they are a passenger in their own vehicle, sitting in the backseat, unable to exert any sense of control over what occurs on the road or, more appropriately, what occurs in their own life. This sensation arises when you realize that you have lost control over some aspects of your life.

The following are some of the factors that might lead to a chakra being blocked and weakened:

Childhood traumas, physical and emotional injuries, having a restricted belief system, cultural conditioning, and poor habits may all produce a blockage in the energy flowing through your chakras, which frequently results in low physical and emotional vitality. Other causes of this blockage include: having a limited belief system; having a limited belief system; having bad habits. The three most prominent factors that contribute to unbalanced and weakened chakras are the emotions of fear, worry, and stress.

Have you recently had the impression that aspects of your life, such as your finances, your personal relationships, or your physical and mental health, have been deteriorating and deteriorating, causing you to experience even more feelings of stress, worry, and frustration? In that case, you may enhance and rebalance all of these parts of your life by working on your chakras. Enhancing the flow of energy to your seven energy centers, also known as chakras, can make you feel much better on both the physical and emotional levels, as well as make a significant contribution to the overall improvement of your well-being, despite the fact that this may seem too simplistic and perhaps too wonderful to be true.

When energy centers are exhausted of their supply of energy, this results in a loss of energy and a decline in well-being. It can be summed up like this.

Going back to the "passenger in your own car" scenario that was given before, if you rebalance your chakras and improve the flow of energy throughout your body, it will be quite easy for you to take control of your life again.

Orange has several advantages, which are referred to as PROS.

• Sociable • Creative • Joyful • Resilient • Self-Reliant

Orange's Downfalls, or CONs, Include the Following:

• Absent; destructive; despondent; destructive; over-dependent

RED

The BASE chakra, which may be found at the bottom of the spine, is governed by the color red. It is associated with the kidneys and bladder, as well as the spinal column, hips, and legs, and it is a symbol of VITALITY, COURAGE, and SELF-CONFIDENCE. Constipation, diarrhea, piles, colitis, Crohn's disease, chilly fingers and toes, frequent urination, hypertension (high blood pressure), kidney stones, impotence, and difficulties of the hips, legs, and feet are some of the health conditions that have been linked to this specific energy center. Red is a symbol of boldness, self-assurance, humanitarianism, strong will, and honesty, as well as the attributes of being spontaneous and extroverted. These are some of the characteristics that are linked with the color red. The color red is associated with having an awareness of oneself, as well as with surviving, being stable, and understanding one's role on earth. The color red gives you strength from the ground up and revitalizes you on all different levels, making it an extremely significant component of your fundamental being.

The advantages (PROS) of the color red

• Safety • Bravery • Dominance of Will • Breaking New Ground

Contraindications (CONS) of the Color Red

- Vulnerability to humiliation of oneself
- Self-pity • Aggression • Fear

THROAT CHAKRA IS THE FIFTH ENERGY CENTER

Stimulating the throat chakra improves our ability to communicate verbally, as well as our respiration, the health of our throat and neck, and our capacity to swallow. Swallowing does not only refer to the act of taking in food or drink; it also refers to taking in the circumstances and the knowledge that we are presented with on a daily basis, as well as digesting (or otherwise accepting) these things.

It will be difficult for the person to let the information in, and as a result, the throat will have difficulties delivering the information if the event, such as the death of a loved one, is too tough for the individual to swallow. If the individual has trouble expressing himself, he may be experiencing discomfort in his throat. The functions listed above are only few of the numerous that the throat is responsible for.

CHAKRA IV: THE HEART CHAKRA

As its name suggests, the heart chakra is associated with the cardiovascular system. A heart that is filled with serenity, love, compassion, and charity is said to have a healthy heart chakra. The individual has a sense of harmony with life, with the circumstances that occur, and with the feelings that are founded on love. It is impossible to love others without first loving oneself.

A heart chakra that is blocked or stuck in one place is a symptom of inner pain, jealously, worry, and melancholy, all of which may lead to feelings of isolation.

The SOLAR PLEXUS CHAKRA is the third chakra.

The solar plexus, which is situated in the middle of the body directly below the ribs, is the third chakra. The kinds of foods we consume and the quantities of those foods also have an impact on this chakra. Additionally, it is common knowledge that the plexus is the optimal location for feelings that have been denied or suppressed. Because of this, when a person is anxious about feeling melancholy, they tend to inhibit their solar plexus.

When we work on opening the chakra located in the solar plexus, it is nearly unavoidable that our emotions will also surface. They go outside to get well. When a chakra is awakened, the energy that travels through it sheds light on things that were before in the dark. The tangles of negative emotions or pollutants are transformed into pure light. In conclusion, the solar chakra is an excellent instructor in accepting oneself and letting go of attachments.

THE SECOND: THE HOLY CHAKRA

The holy chakra has a close connection to one's life energy as well as their sense of taste, desire, pleasure, inventiveness, and sexual organs. One may determine the state of one's chakra by looking at the desires that they have.

The desire to take care of oneself, to have a healthy sexual life, to maintain excellent eating habits are all examples of healthy wants. Love, sensitivity, and appreciation are all related concepts here.

An overactive chakra, which may lead to excessiveness, or a chakra that isn't active enough, which can lead to sadness, can both play a role in stimulating unhealthy urges. Unhealthy urges include things like using drugs or smoking, having sexual dysfunction or having insignificant sex, spending money in gaming, and even overeating. These things, among many other repercussions, lead to possessiveness, difficulty in disillusioning oneself, discontent, and a lack of. These difficulties help us get to the truth in a hurry.

TO START, THE ROOT CHAKRA

The root chakra is the connection point between our spiritual selves and the physical, material universe. The energy of the root chakra is in constant communication with the gravitational core of the planet. This chakra's light is red, and it serves to ground and stabilize us. To maintain a healthy existence as a person on this planet, it is necessary to have roots. On the other hand, having too much of a foothold in one place might cause us to lose touch with the unseen world, which is just as significant as the visible one. We have to find a middle ground between the two.

In addition, this chakra is associated with the fundamental requirements of the human body. In the same way as the holy chakra, there may be an excess of it when it is stimulated too much. This excess may manifest itself in the form of food, drink, financial wealth, sexual activity, or consumerism. An open and healthy root chakra has a natural tendency to produce a variety of beneficial benefits, including a sense of safety, a greater appreciation for the here and now, and a stronger connection to the planet.

The Seven Mantras for Purification

LAM is a cleaning mantra that is repeated for the Root Chakra. Chanting this mantra helps one remain rooted in the soil and connected to it. By chanting this mantra, impurities that have been held in the root chakra will be cleansed, which will actually open you up to emotions of security, prosperity, and belonging. Additionally, any blocked energy that has hindered a person from going upwards to the other six primary energy centers will also be cleared. Chant "LAM" if you feel like your energy is low, if you are having financial difficulties, if you have poor self-esteem, if you have adrenal exhaustion, or if you suffer from any other stress-related diseases.

VAM: This is a purifying mantra for the Sacral Chakra, which is connected to sexuality, pleasure, and creativity. The activation of this chakra will make you more receptive to other people, as well as offer you the confidence and bravery to express who you are and to welcome change. Chant "VAM" if you suffer from low libido, have a negative self-image, or find it difficult to be expressive in your interactions with people and family in general.

RAM: This purifying mantra awakens the Solar Plexus Chakra, which is the basis of your own strength. Chanting "RAM" will strengthen your capacity to stand up for yourself, handle bad urges, and exhibit better self-control than you would otherwise have. As you continue to chant "RAM," you will see an increase in both your self-esteem and your level of self-assurance and confidence. If you suffer from regular stomach aches and worry, you will find that reciting this mantra helps reduce both of those symptoms.

YAM: The purification mantra for the Heart Chakra is as follows. Through the energy axis that is located in our heart chakra, we are able to both offer and receive love with one another. If we are not feeling loving, amicable, or sympathetic, or if we are going through a difficult time in our relationships, we might chant YAM! Chanting "YAM" heals both the physical heart as well as the spiritual (emotional) heart center, opens us up to unconditional love and compassion, and helps us open up to these feelings more fully.

HAM: The goal of this purifying mantra is to clear any obstructions from the Throat Chakra. This is both the physical and spiritual voice of our people, as well as the mechanism by which we communicate who we are and what we want from you and the universe. If we do not have the capacity to express ourselves, which comes from having a blocked throat chakra, we will discover that we are constantly irritated, which will cause us to shut ourselves off to opportunities and prevent us from getting our needs fulfilled. Additionally, having a closed throat chakra will make it difficult to demonstrate honesty and integrity. The vibrations from "RAM" will expand our throat chakra, allowing for a more powerful flow of energy associated with speech.

This purifying chant, referred to as AUM (or OM), awakens the Third Eye Chakra. This point is located in the middle of the forehead, just in the middle of the crease that separates the eyebrows. In spite of the fact that OM is one of the most well-known mantras and that it is used extensively during mantra meditations, it is of utmost significance for the purpose of purifying and repairing the third eye chakra. The third eye chakra is where one's intuition and sense of life's purpose are magnified. By not letting oneself to listen to their own inner knowledge and using that insight to design the best route for a life of purpose and passion, a person may have unintentionally put some limitations upon themselves. Chanting "OM" will help a person break free from these limitations and set them free.

These purifying mantras, such as OM or AH, are for the Crown Chakra, which is the connection to the divine. A blocked crown chakra causes a person to experience emotions of insignificance and worthlessness, which in turn leads to a detachment from the spirit realm and an unhealthy preoccupation with material goods, interpersonal connections, and the external world. Some people believe that practicing stillness is the most effective way to awaken the crown chakra, while others believe that chanting OM may also have that impact. A release is indicated by chanting the letter 'AH'. Imagine drawing a full breath in and then letting it out all at once. The sound of letting go and surrendering oneself is represented by the letter AH.

A Color Therapy Approach To Restoring Chakra Balance

Chromotherapy is another name for this method, which includes using different colors to bring each of the chakras into harmony with one another.

Your chakras' energy system is sensitive to the effects of all of the colors in the rainbow's spectrum, each in its own unique way. This is because different colors have different wavelengths, which results in this phenomenon. Each hue exudes a certain kind of energy that resonates with a particular major chakra located inside the human body.

Therefore, you may utilize color therapy to bring your chakras back into alignment by applying the proper colors to various parts of your body.

The following is a list of some easy strategies you may use to achieve healing via the use of colors:

Utilization of solid colors for the textiles

Your primary chakras may be brought back into balance and your radiant energy can be enhanced by doing this simple exercise. Because it is so simple and you can carry it out all by yourself, this is something that can be done on a regular basis. You only need to get several square items of clothing in a variety of chakra colors, and then you should proceed as follows:

1. Locate a calm, distraction-free location where you may concentrate on this activity for a maximum of ten to fifteen minutes.

2. Place a mat on the floor and lie down on your back on it. Bring out the seven items of clothing in your closet that have hues that correspond to the seven primary chakras. That consists of the colors (red, violet, orange, green, indigo, yellow, and blue).

3. With your eyes closed, bring your attention to the present now, relax your body and mind, and take numerous calm, deep breaths for around five minutes.

4. While you are in a state of relaxation, think back on everything that has happened during the day, beginning with the most recent occurrence and working your way all the way back to the beginning of the day. Make sure that you go over every aspect of the previous day in detail.

5. Recognize and name all of the different feelings and attitudes that you experienced during the day. Locate the chakras that may have been harmed as a result of the aforementioned thoughts and feelings.

6. Once you have completed the appropriate examination, take the piece of cloth that corresponds to the wounded chakra and lay it on the area of the body that contains that chakra.

7. While you are still laying on your back and the colored swatch is still placed on top of the chakra point, close your eyes and attempt to imagine that the color from the fabric is being sucked into your body and absorbed by that specific chakra. You need to bring your attention back into focus and process the fact that the balancing of your chakras is now occurring, as well as the fact that all of the bodily organs and systems associated with that chakra are also becoming balanced. You should do this as soon as possible.

8. While you concentrate on bringing that hue from the fabric swatch into your chakra, be sure to take a few long, deep breaths to assist you in bringing your chakras into a state of equilibrium.

Meditation on the Heart Chakra 3

The use of music is essential in order to restore health to the chest and heart region.

Begin by selecting a tune with a soothing melody, one that has pleasant rhythms and noises but no words, since this will prevent you from singing along in your brain.

It has been shown via research that listening to the appropriate kind of music may improve one's mood, thus it is important to look for songs or albums to which one has an emotional connection.

Turn it on by a few bars so that it is audible but not too loud, for example, by turning it on at one-fourth of the way through the music bars.

Be sure that the song lasts for at least 10 minutes, or play it again and over again.

First, choose a comfortable position to lie down in and let yourself to unwind.

If you want the maximum amount of comfort, put a cushion under your head and another one under your legs.

Place your palms facing up next to your body while your hands are laying down close to your body.

Take a moment to bring your attention within and clear your thoughts by taking several deep breaths.

Take a deep breath in via your nose, pause to hold it for two seconds, and then let it out through your mouth.

Keep using this simple and easy breathing method for the next minute.

While you focus on relaxing your body as much as you can while you inhale through your nose and exhale through your mouth, you should try to relax your body as much as you can.

The next step is to slowly close your eyes while directing all of your focus on the region around your chest.

When you breathe, breathe out through your chest rather than through your stomach.

This indicates that when you take a breath in, you should give your lungs room to expand so that they may begin to move around and fill with oxygen.

Make sure that you are focusing all of your attention on your chest, specifically how it expands and contracts as you breathe in and out, as well as how the rest of your body either becomes larger as you breathe in or becomes smaller as you breathe out.

Imagine that with each breath you take, you are able to purge the negative energy from your chest, expelling it out your mouth as you do so, and enabling yourself to let go of any tensions or impurities that may be weighing you down.

As you continue to let your body relax and as you grow more used to the rhythm of your body's deep breathing, start paying close attention to the many melodies that you hear and make an effort to zero in on one in particular that sticks out to you. This will help you become more comfortable with the rhythm of your body's deep breathing.

For instance, if the sound of the bells is what you hear, then direct your attention on the sound of the bells.

While you listen to that calm and soothing music, you should make an effort to push any thoughts that may be arising to the back of your brain and instead focus on relaxing.

Take a minute to savor the sound of the music that you are now listening to.

Consider how this tune makes you feel on an emotional level. Are you experiencing joy and love in your heart? If yes, continue by imagining your heart beating faster and faster, as if it were becoming more receptive to love.

Imagine that your heart is a flower whose petals are opening out and floating all around you, waiting to be sent out to your loved ones.

Maintain contact with your own experience of love, and link that experience to the petals of the flower.

Think of a person who is important to you, such as a friend, a lover, or a member of your family, and imagine sending them dazzling pink or green petals, full with the love and compassion that you feel for them.

I hope they are blessed with joy and success throughout their lives.

Imagine those petals moving to wherever they are at the moment and making contact with their hearts as they do so.

Participate in this activity with two or three additional individuals who have a special place in your heart.

Feel the warmth and tingle as more petals emerge from your heart and make their way to the people you care about.

Allow the energy that has been building up in your heart to flow out into the rest of your body; while you do so, feel love spreading throughout your whole being.

Allow the energy to flow freely up and down your spine via all of your chakras, bringing them together and fostering your development on a spiritual level.

Step one is to set your purpose to bring the energy back to the surface, and step two is to consult the cosmos for direction on this exercise.

Keep your concentration on the white auric field that encircles your body and helps you to feel secure and at ease.

You will start to experience tingling sensations all over your body, along with a warm feeling.

Allow the healing energy to slowly resurface throughout your body and allow it to focus on the location of your heart. This will help it to work more effectively.

As you continued to do the exercise of releasing petals, your heart got more cheerful and pure, which made it simpler for the energy to enter and move through it.

Put forth the desire to be protected against everything unfavorable that may occur in your life, including unfavorable experiences, unfavorable feelings, and unfavorable individuals.

Because of this, you will feel more protected and at peace in the face of adversity.

Set another intention with the goal of getting self-healing energy, this time focusing on the chest area of your body.

Permit that energy to go from your heart to your shoulders and then down to the palms of your hands, all the while maintaining a connection with one another while it does so.

You should direct your energy onto your hands and focus on using them as a focal point for it.

It is important that you allow the flow of white energy to reappear in your hands so that they may radiate a pure white tone.

Spend a moment simply allowing all of the energy to catch up and collect in one location, and in the process, heal the hands as it works its way through the body.

Raise both of your hands to your chest and rest them there, overlapping one on top of the other.

Permit the energy to permeate your heart chakra, and in your mind's eye, see the white light transform into the vibrant green hue that is linked with the heart chakra.

Put your attention on feeling the beat of your heart against your palms, and focus on sensing the pulsating sensations that are occurring below.

Take a deep breath and try to relax as you feel the green light go deeper into your chest.

Permit the energy to go freely around the chest region and investigate it, directing it to go precisely where tension is present.

Feel the tingling sensations all over your body, smell the air around you as you take in deep breaths, hear the soft melody echoing in the room or against your ears, taste the freedom and love that life gives you, and finally, notice the glowing green light emerging through your heart even though your eyes are closed.

Imagine the color burning stronger and brighter as it opens your heart chakra to all of the love and happiness that you rightfully deserve. This will help you feel more connected to the world.

Think back on the many occasions on which love was shown to you and given to you; remember that even the little things that brought you joy still matter.

Make room in your heart for the mending that you need.

To assist you in opening this chakra even more, use the mantra "yam."

Invest some time and energy into opening your chakra. Don't try to speed through the process; instead, give your body the time it needs to mend its heart on a physical or emotional level.

To finish, take several minutes to concentrate only on the music and the range of sensations that it elicits in you as you take slow, deep breaths in through your mouth and out through your nose.

The purpose of this meditation is to fill your chest region with good and unadulterated energy while also making you experience love for life, love for others around you, and most importantly, love for yourself.

When you reach the point where you believe you are done, stop what you are doing and let the energy settle into your body for a minute or two.

Allow your eyes to gradually acclimate to the light and the environment around you as you allow them to open gradually.

Be sure to give some thought to the healing that has come to you as a result of the meditation that you have just finished doing.

Step one is to get started by engaging in an activity that brings you pleasure or that you like.

After the healing process is complete, give yourself permission to rest and don't hurry yourself to go back to normal.

Stay in, take it easy, soak in a warm bath, and give your body time to mend itself while the energy that is still inside it.

The Exchange Of Chakra Energies Between Two Different People

Each chakra has its own unique way of being articulated, and they each represent a distinct aspect of existence. When two individuals come together in any kind of relationship, there is also a chakra connection that is made between them. The energy comes in from the right side, and the left side of the chakra is where it is accepted. This is how the chakra is able to provide. When anything like this takes place, the stream will continue to be changed. Regardless of this, it's not absolutely necessary that the transmission be perfect all of the time. It is possible that there is a corresponding obstruction in at least one of the chakras. The great correspondence is exacerbated if the chakra of the sender is blocked, damaged, or either underactive or hyperactive. Representing chakras, engaging in recuperative practices, meditating, and engaging in breathing exercises that focus on chakras are all excellent ways to correct any blockages, injuries, or activations that may have occurred.

What a remarkable connection it creates between two individuals when their chakras correspond to one another:

The Sacral Chakra is the chakra associated with joy, creativity, and being assured of oneself. In addition to that, it is associated with dread, a need for self-preservation, and an insatiable appetite.

When a pair communicates via the sacral chakra, it results in an attachment that is susceptible to comfort and wealth. They will probably live a nice life, with a lovely house full of gorgeous furnishings, and a pristine and amazing automobile parked in front of their home. They need to work together in order to accomplish what they want.

This chakra is connected with the fundamental senses and is impacted by sexual energy. It is located at the base of the spine. The survival nature chakra is the one that provides the impetus to go on living. It also has a connection to one's conscience as well as their childlike nature. The pair who is aligned with their root chakra values the organization that each other brings to the relationship.

The Solar Plexus Chakra: This chakra is related to the energy chakras that are present in the light body. It is also compared to desires, goals, and material delights. These couples have autonomy from a young age and enjoy the opportunity to participate in games and contests with one another. Accolade and prominence are both essential to their success.

The principal chakra beneath the larger quantity of energy focuses that inspire a healthy connection is the one located in the center of the chest, known as the heart chakra. These couples want to live together in happiness and tranquility, and they need such things for one another.

The Throat Chakra: Individuals whose beliefs are influenced by the throat chakra have a responsibility to develop their faculties. These two people are really religious. They find inner calm via meditative practices. They become more trustworthy and confident as time goes on. They should just give thought to the idea of realizing their superior selves rather than rely on their normal sensations.

People who are associated with the third eye chakra engage in acts of self-acknowledgment on a regular basis. Their deep and meaningful connection compels them to sacrifice their life for the sake of the enjoyment of others. Their primary goal is to find contentment and tranquility. When they are together, they need to practice being faultless with one another and have a shared interest in learning about the universe. Their relationship is one that is more spiritual in nature as opposed to sexual.

The Crown Chakra

The crown chakra is associated with a kind of love that is otherworldly and wonderful. These couples have absolutely no desire for sexual activity; rather, it is just a must for maintaining their romantic connection.

The Phrase "Manipura" The Solar Plexus Chakra, Often Known As The Sun Energy Center

The element of fire is represented by the Manipura. It is connected to our perception of color and our eyesight. This chakra may be situated on either the solar plexus or the gastrointestinal area of the umbilicus. This chakra has an effect on a person's feeling of well-being as well as their capacity to comprehend and work through emotional challenges, as well as their stamina, willpower, and ego. A manipura charka that is out of balance may have a variety of negative effects on a person. These conditions include diabetes, arthritis, stomach discomfort and ulcers, low blood pressure, low self-esteem, depression, inability to make choices, animosity, and bad decision making skills. Others include poor decision making abilities and poor decision making abilities. Anger and fits of wrath are also experienced by certain individuals. A person who has achieved chakra balance has an abundance of vitality, as well as the self-assurance and shrewdness necessary to make sound judgments. When this chakra is functioning properly, it paves the way for excellent mental concentration, improved digestive health, and increased productivity throughout the day. It is thought that the essential oils of rosemary and lavender, among others, might help to strengthen this chakra.

The Solar Plexus, also known as the Manipura Chakra, is responsible for a variety of emotional issues, including a lack of vitality, poor self-esteem, and a negative self-image. It is also possible for it to produce rage, the want to be more powerful than another person, as well as the desire to be flawless in all respects. This may lead to the development of depression in addition to the individual's demand for stimulants. Participating in yoga practices, particularly those that target the third chakra, such as the Half

Boat Pose, Leg Lifts, and the Boat Pose, is extremely useful for this chakra.

This chakra, which is located just above the navel, is responsible for regulating the functions of the upper abdomen, including the liver, pancreas, middle spine, gall bladder, adrenals, kidney, spleen, stomach, and small intestine.

Your self-confidence, development, and ability to exercise self-control, as well as your sense of humor, self-power, and ego power, are all impacted by the chakra. When this chakra is out of whack, it may lead to a number of health problems, including diabetes, constipation, digestive troubles, ulcers, concerns with one's self-esteem, an extreme sensitivity to criticism, worries related to one's own self-image, anxiousness, and poor memory.

Your self-respect is determined by the Manipura chakra. The solar plexus chakra is where mental awareness, ego, optimism, will strength, and self-assurance are born. Your capacity to focus your attention and your awareness on particular details is controlled by the energy center known as the chakra. This chakra is where your innate inclinations are channeled.

The Third Eye Chakra Allows One To See

The third eye chakra, also known as "Ajna" in Sanskrit, is also known as "beyond wisdom." The sixth chakra is the hub of foresight or intuition, and it symbolizes psychic energy or intuition, extra-sensory perception, the capacity to think, decision-making, imagination, wisdom, and any other information that is not received via the five senses. It broadens the intellect to include a universe that exists beyond the physical or material reality. We all have a natural capacity for intuition, but not all of us listen to it or heed the cautions it provides. Awakening this chakra will assist us in developing this skill further.

The third eye chakra may be found in the middle of the forehead, just in the middle of the brows. The fundamental rule of openness and creativity guides the operation of this system. The sixth chakra is shown by an inverted triangle and a lotus flower, both of which are connected with the quality of knowledge. This chakra is represented by the color purple or a blue purple.

This chakra extends far beyond the realm of the physical senses and into the realm of the subtle energies. Because everyone of us has a unique way of seeing and understanding the world around us, it may be challenging to properly convey the visuals. It offers us the opportunity to develop a stronger connection with the intangible.

In order to restore harmony to the third eye chakra, we have to see through the pretense that we are separate from one another. Even though we are all a part of a same entity, we behave as if we are separate. To comprehend complete liberty, one must first realize that different manifestations of the same energy make up each one of us.

The Third Eye Chakra and Other Non-Traditional Methods of Healing

Indigo or violet; any hue

The element that is light

Position: In the middle of the forehead, between the brows

Disturbances of Emotional Health Caused by Blockages: Symptoms may include anxiety, despair, inability to hear one's own inner voice, difficulty focusing, difficulty sleeping, nightmares, obsessions, and delusions.

Ailments of the body resulting from Blockages: Vision or eye difficulties, a predisposition to headaches and sinus problems.

Crystals as a Medium for Healing: tiger iron, rainbow fluorite, moonstone, lapis lazuli, purple fluorite, hawk's eye, ceylon sapphire, amethyst, and amethyst sapphire, amethyst, amethyst, amethyst

Spruce, St. John's wort, and Euphrasia are Some Medicinal Herbs That Can Help You Get Well.

Recovery with the use of the Bach Flower Method: Grape, hazelnut, and crab apple

Cajeput, lemongrass, and violet essential oils are used therapeutically for healing.

Chanting the sound "OM" (the universal seed sound), a healing modality, may help.

Affirmations for healing: "I trust my inner voice" "I see clearly and let my inner light shine"

Activating the Chakra of the Third Eye: Practice meditation outside beneath the night sky, maintain a dream diary, read books on spirituality, and familiarize yourself with the ideas and writings of some of history's most influential thinkers and philosophers.

Meditation and yoga pose known as the Child's Pose

The Philosophy BehindTantra and Yoga

When it first arose in the 10th century, Tantra completely rethought the notion of yoga. It was a methodical approach to life that is similar to the way Hinduism and Buddhism see the world and its purpose. It is the study of, and the practice of, the manner in which the body is able to let the prana to go through you, as well as the manner in which you will be able to perceive all of the motions that it makes. The term "kundalini" refers to both the movement of the energy as well as the course that it travels. This movement and path illustrate the many ways in which it is possible to synchronize one's own awareness with that of the cosmos.

Tantra is the technique of bringing the energy up through the chakras in the body, from one to the next, and activating them in such a way that the individual may become perfectly connected with the cosmos and linked in to it.

The usage and practice of activating the chakras was a hidden technique that was taught in a variety of covert locales. This was done to guarantee that only a very small number of individuals were aware of how to do the activation procedure. In literature, secret cults may be traced all the way back to the sixth century BC. These cults met in secluded areas and conducted their religion in secret so that they would not be bothered by the demands of the outside world.

The Definition of Charkas

It has been said that they resemble a lotus rather than a wheel; when one chakra is activated, it enables the meditator to reach a new degree of consciousness as well as a new level of connection with the cosmos. These are the fundamental aspects of the chakras.

The Muladhara Chakra, often known as the Root Chakra, consists of:

The first chakra serves as the physical, vital, and ancestral root of our being. It may be found near the base of the coccyx, in the space between the anus and the genitals, and its role in the body is connected to the robustness of the bones, teeth, and nails, as well as the gut, legs, and feet. However, this has a psychological, physical, and emotional expression since, in some way, the Muladhara chakra is the energy center that somehow feeds us with vital vitality. It is the energy that is responsible for the development of the other chakras. This is the location of the kundalini, the cosmic energy that is associated with the tantric tradition. Additionally, the Sushumna, Ida, and Pingala energy channels all start at this point, making the first chakra the epicenter of the subtle energy medicine cycle.

This chakra is the one that is most closely aligned with our animal and tribal nature. Although it is farther removed from our transcendent being, it is just as lovely as the things that are more spiritual since it represents our most fundamental self and our connection to the earth as a source of life, strength, and protection. It is also the drive that wants our survival, which drives us to act, but also gives us the fundamental fire to work every day. These are all aspects of the same underlying drive. It is not simply as a primal rhythm; rather, it is exhibited via confidence and warmth body-mind from where capacity for action, creativity, self-esteem, and fundamental drive show off. It is a significant factor that brings about the process of establishing our roots, constructing, and looking for stability.

As the momentum that gives us life, and ontological security, confidence, and power, it is a vital aspect of our being and relates to the key part of our wellness. This energy refers to our physical state, which includes being linked with the land and the natural surroundings as well as our body as a manifestation of the earth and listening to their need.

The red that defines itself as the same hue as the most fundamental energy of the planet and, by extension, of life that originates from it. Additionally, it is the hue of blood. Our instinctual plane, which is associated with the first chakra, requires a sense of security in the areas of food, clothes, and shelter; it also ensures that their well-being is protected. Because this is the group root that provides us with a feeling of belonging and a psychological location, in addition to including a map of mental and emotional safety, this has multiple aspects beyond the physical. But if we look at it from a physical standpoint, we see that this being is also connected to the natural cycles that the body goes through and the requirements that it has in order to develop its potential and its vitality.

The Significance Of The Chakras

Each of the seven chakras has a bundle of nerves, which are essential to our physical, mental, and emotional health. Chakras are located at certain points along the spine. Because of this, the chakras are an essential component of our health and the way in which we are able to experience life. Our chakras need to be correctly aligned, open, and flexible in order to enable the energy to flow easily through our bodies. This is because the energy is always in motion, and because of this, the energy must be able to move freely through our bodies. Permit me to illustrate this point by referring to the bathtub that is located in your master bathroom. If you clean it too often, the hair may accumulate in the drain, causing water to pool in the tub and encouraging the development of mildew, fungus, and viruses. This might happen if you clean it too frequently. This is the exact way that our body functions, with the exception that the chakras are not physically present in the same way that your bathtub's drain is, and thus cannot be simply rectified.

However, if you let yourself to be conscious, you may guarantee that all of your chakras are open at all times. Because you lack awareness, you are unable to comprehend the factors that contribute to the inactivity of your chakras. Take, for instance, the tale of a person who has just suffered the loss of a loved one. He ends up with bronchitis, and as a result of his coughing, he has discomfort in his chest every time he coughs. However, if the individual is unable to make the connection between the death of a loved one due to bronchitis and his inability to open his chakras, the connection will remain unmade. If he does, then he will acknowledge and respect the mourning process, and he will treat it alongside the physical problem that he is currently dealing with. As a result, he will recover much more quickly. Therefore, being aware of the chakras is a necessary step toward activating a chakra that is now dormant.

Methods Of Breathing That Will Assist You In Keeping Your Chakras Open

The utilization of one's belly to transmit more energy and awareness is key to the most efficient practices, such as the "belly breathing" method. If you are able to learn and perfect this method, it will be beneficial to your overall wellbeing and health.

You will also discover that it is not simply the act of breathing itself that is significant, but also the ability to recall how to breathe well. The intention to maximize the advantages that come with the correct use of breathing methods should be the primary point of emphasis here. During the practice, it is essential to bring your awareness to the breath, since this is the single most critical factor in determining how well your mind, physical body, and soul are all able to function.

It is a beneficial practice that will assist you to enhance your health, boost your vitality, and bring greater awareness to your body. Belly breathing allows you to do all of these things.

What exactly does the belly breathing technique entail?

Put the tips of your index fingers and thumbs together, then position them just below your navel or in the region of your second chakra that is right above the area of your pubic region. Imagine that you are breathing in and out while touching this place. When you breathe into your belly, you'll experience a richer and more profound sense of breath. In addition to that, it will assist you in providing your breath with the ideal direction. When you are laying down or standing up, it is much simpler to breathe into your stomach than of your chest. You may also practice while seated, however it is more difficult since you can end up filling your chest rather than your belly.

Pay attention to how you are breathing to ensure that you are inflating your stomach rather than your chest.

It is a frequent and natural mental image to see one's breath travelling from the lower abdomen to the upper chest, then to the crown, and finally out of the tops of our heads. It is for this reason why, when we breathe deeply, we elevate our chests to allow more air into our lungs so that they may become fully saturated. We often learn to soothe our nervous systems and significantly cut down on tension and worry.

When you breathe in through your nose and out through your mouth, however, you release all of your positive energy, also known as prana, into the surrounding air. If you breathe out, you won't be able to reap the benefits of strengthening your chakras. You may opt to breathe out if you feel that your chakras are already powerful and well balanced. If this is the case, it's perfectly OK.

NOTE: To practice belly breathing, picture exhaling through your mouth and then do the opposite. Instead of taking a big breath in and then releasing it, try drawing your breath inwards and downwards, then drawing it all the way into your stomach.

In some situations, there are those who breathe deeply from the chest, while others breathe from the abdomen. If you consider yourself to be someone who breathes deeply from the chest, you should aim to minimize the amount that you elevate your chest when you breathe. As you let your breath out, your tummy should fall in. At first, it may not be easy, but putting in more practice will help you become more proficient with the method. It is also OK for you to elevate your chest; however, you should make sure that your abdominal muscles are working quickly.

Some individuals have a propensity to clutch their bellies, particularly when they are motivated by the desire to seem to be thinner than they really are. They are unaware that they are harboring powerful emotions in the region of their belly, which leads to issues with the second chakra later on. The harboring of sentiments that are not acceptable is situated deep inside the center of our selves. These suppressed and unrecognized feelings will eventually manifest themselves in our bodies as illnesses if they are not dealt with.

persons who have been through traumatic experiences may find it challenging, frightening, or unpleasant to practice belly breathing. It is crucial for persons who are having problems practicing belly breathing to get expert therapy.

Instructions to Help You Get Started Practicing Belly Breathing

To begin, take a deep breath in and try to bring it all the way down into your belly. Focus your attention on the rise and fall of your belly. Additionally, you may direct your attention on the hands that you had put on the belly rise earlier. It is not necessary for you to put your hands in your belly if you continue practicing, but if you find that the exercise is more enjoyable with your hands there, feel free to keep them there.

Make sure that you are keeping your breath in your belly as you exhale and your hands and belly go lower towards your spine; this indicates that you are holding your breath there. Avoid letting your prana leave your body and instead focus on drawing the vital energy into your being.

pretend that you are stocking a shop with each breath that you take, and then pretend that you are expelling while keeping the breath that is still in your abdomen. This will allow you to quickly fill your belly and will also help you to fill it more completely.

And these are all of the stages that are essential for you to master in order to properly do the belly breathing methods. Always make sure that you have completed at least 10 breaths in order to properly recuperate. If you are used to the shallow breaths of yoga, switching to belly breathing might be difficult at first since you are used to taking in a smaller volume of oxygen. You may just give your usual breathing pattern a try and work on practicing belly breathing as the days go by.

You should make it a point to practice belly breathing at least once or twice a day, but particularly when you feel like both your body and mind are dragging. You will notice a difference in yourself as well as an increase in your overall energy levels as a result of this activity.

The Shyness of Leo

Being true to oneself was extremely challenging for Leo while interacting with other people, particularly females. Since he broke up with his girlfriend Sarah when he was 23 years old, which was a difficult experience in and of itself, he has been struggling with an ever-growing phobia of intimacy.

It was a difficult split for Leo. Since the end of their senior year of high school, he had been in a committed relationship with Sarah, during which time they had built not just a robust sexual life but also a solid emotional connection. When Sarah admitted that she had cheated on Leo with his best friend, it caused Leo's level of self-confidence and faith in women to collapse, and he found it exceedingly difficult to believe that the same thing would not happen again. Sarah's admission caused Leo to cheat on Leo with his best buddy. As a direct consequence of this, his sexual life vanished completely.

Due to the fact that Leo is unable to express himself sexually and in an intimate environment, he is unable to be confident in a variety of social contexts. These settings include his place of employment as well as public areas. When he is among women who seem to be attracted to him, he often has self-doubts, second-guesses his judgments, and errs on the side of caution because he is afraid of being rejected or, even worse, of being accepted but taken advantage of. Leo's lack of self-assurance and his present perspective on sexuality tend to go in the way of him having the satisfying sexual experience he craves with a woman with whom he has a mutual intellectual and physical affinity; nonetheless, this is the one thing he wants more than anything else in the world. In an effort to alleviate his inferiority complex, Leo gives in to destructive behaviors and addictions such as masturbation, binge drinking, and binge watching television. He constantly questions how he might improve the situation.

Dave, a mutual acquaintance of Leo's, had extended an invitation to a party with a Cuban theme to him one weekend. Because of his tendency, he immediately responded with a negative response when you considered that he connected events of this kind with high levels of energy and powerful women who were certain in their sexuality. On this particular occasion, Leo, on the other hand, was in the mood for a drink and gladly accepted the offer. He went to the party wearing his go-to orange flannel shirt and then got into the car. After arriving, he looked for his buddy but was unsuccessful, so he headed straight to the bar to get a drink and mull over the fact that he would in all likelihood have to spend some time there before meeting up with Dave. However, as Leo was making his way through the sea of Cuba Libres that was floating among the bright grins and sundresses, he saw that the party was decorated in an orange motif. Orange was the color of the little umbrellas that came with Old Cuban drinks. The majority of the ladies were dressed in orange. In addition, the decorations had a warm, tropical orange hue to them.

When Leo arrived to the pub, he was thinking about the coincidence and ran into a very stunning lady. Despite her good looks, however, what first caught Leo's attention was the startling intellect that could be seen in her eyes. After offering an apology, Leo turned his attention back to the beverages on the table. The woman approached him and initiated a chat. Leo started to loosen up a little bit as soon as he had his drink, and he began to truly start enjoying the company of the lady who appeared to have a lot in common with him. She identified herself as Stacy when she first spoke. He saw that she was enjoying his company as much as he did, and as a result, he began to feel more at ease in her presence.

After a short period of time, Leo's body language started sending out positive vibes. He was standing with his back to Stacy, but his eyes were bright with a smile, and his voice was louder and more assured than before. Stacy was aware of this, and she responded with the same kind of energy that she had received. She dropped a hint that she was interested in spending some time with him once the celebration was over. Leo had reached the point when he chose to let go of his expectations about the nature of the connection that should exist between himself and a woman and instead focus on living in the present. After Leo and Stacy developed a strong friendship with one another, they planned to get together the next weekend.

During that get-together, Stacy revealed to Leo that she had observed him to be feeling a little depressed when they first met at the party, despite the fact that at first he gave the impression of being a carefree, fun-loving person. Leo filled her in on his predicament, especially focusing on the fact that ever since he had broken up with his ex-girlfriend, he had been feeling low and unhappy. Leo's confidence was significantly bolstered as a result of Stacy's reiteration of the fact that she never in a million years would have suspected that he had an issue of any kind. Before they had that discussion, Leo was under the impression that other people could pick up on the fact that something was different with him, and this was hampering his capacity to build connections with other people. It demonstrated that what is happening on the inside may not always be reflected on the exterior, and one must not automatically assume that just because they are experiencing negative emotions that everyone else will notice it. Communication is essential, and while Leo didn't understand it at the time, his inability to communicate effectively had been an issue for much longer than he thought. It would have been much simpler and faster to solve things and it would not have taken as much time for him to get out of the rut that he was in, or at least the rut that he imagined he was in, if he had just shared his emotions at an earlier point in time.

In this particular illustration, Leo went from being someone who had a blocked sacral chakra to successfully taking the first step toward opening it and bringing it back into balance by actively connecting with and enabling his creative side to blossom in the present now. The good energy that was sent out by his sacral chakra was finally repaid by the cosmos in the form of a fortunate meeting with a woman who he has a very strong connection with. He has conquered the unpleasant feelings that have plagued him over the previous two years and managed to steer clear of their clutches.

Asanas pertaining to the Sacral Chakra in Yoga

In order to properly meditate on the sacral chakra, you need to give your creative side some attention. The sacral chakra may be stimulated and encouraged to foster creative expression via a variety of activities, including but not limited to dancing, composing music, and painting. The Butterfly posture, also known as BaddhaKonasana, is considered to be the most effective yoga position for developing this chakra's power. However, there are numerous other positions that may help develop this chakra's strength.

Take a seat on the floor with your legs crossed. It is recommended that you try pressing the soles of your feet against each other if you are flexible enough to do so. After then, bring your left hand over to the other side of your body and place it there. Maintain this posture by putting your right hand over your left wrist and keeping it there. As you bend down and make an effort to place your forehead on the ground, take a deep breath in and then let it out. Maintain the stance for eight seconds, then bring your body into a vertical position while taking a deep breath in.

You need to keep your attention focused on your sacral chakra as you hold the position. Make an effort to direct the energy that is coursing through your body to the region around your navel. You are already sending blood to that place, therefore the energy will travel with your blood as it makes its way there. Physically speaking. As a result of the fact that this chakra is referred to as the 'sex' chakra, practicing this meditation is supposed to assist with conception, menstruation, and reproductive actions in general.

The low lunge is another position that works on opening the sacral chakra.

After getting into a standing position, bring your right leg as far forward as you can while keeping your left knee on the ground to maintain balance. Put your palms together, arch your back slightly, and elevate your arms and head up into the heavens while you do this exercise. At the same time that you are extending your front leg forward, exhale, and continue to exhale once you have completed the position. The procedure of inhaling and exhaling should be repeated for a total of five breaths while you concentrate on opening your sacral chakra.

The triangle position is the next one for working on opening up the sacral chakra. Assuming that your legs are separated by the width of one shoulder, lean to one side while keeping your arms spread out horizontally and parallel to the ground. Lean to one side as far as you comfortably can, then repeat on the other side while maintaining an upright face position. Your whole body should be relaxed, and you should focus on your breathing while directing energy towards the position of your sacral chakra.

The goddess posture is the following one in the sequence. Begin by spreading your legs apart, and then bend both knees until they form a right angle (90 degrees). In a similar manner, position your arms so that they form an angle of 90 degrees with your body and point your palms toward the ceiling. While you are in this position, be sure to hold the root chakra's mundra. While you are holding the posture, exhale, and then while you are exiting the stance, inhale. While you are holding this position, try to bring your attention to the process of opening your sacral chakra.

The wide-angle sitting forward bend is the next position to be practiced after the goddess pose. While seated on your buttocks, try to spread your legs as far apart as you can and lean forward. Place the top of your head on the floor and bring both arms up to meet over your head with your hands interlaced. Imagine that you are fully present in this moment and that you are directing your energy to the region around your navel, where the sacral chakra is situated.

Pigeon position is the next posture you may practice to activate the sacral chakra, and it's a good one to start with. Because of your proximity to the ground and the emphasis placed on the region surrounding your navel, energy might be directed onto your sacral chakra when you assume this posture. From your knees, bend forward with one knee tucked below your chest and the other knee spread out in front of you. Start by doing this. Hold the knee that is tucked under your chest with the hand that corresponds to that knee, and rest your forehead on the hand that is not holding your knee. While you are in this posture, exhale, and then as soon as you return to a vertical position, inhale. Continue this method for approximately a minute while directing your attention on the region around your navel.

How The Seven Chakras Affect Our Everyday Lives

Because chakras serve as energy "plug-in points" and "transportation hubs," the area of the body that they are located in immediately influences them, and they in turn are directly impacted by that area, in the same way that you are influenced by your surroundings. Because of this, a chakra's state of health has an effect on the area of your body in which it is located, and vice versa; the interaction is mutually beneficial and symbiotic.

Both scientific research in the field of medicine and anecdotal evidence demonstrate that our tissues and muscles often function as the hard drives of our bodies, storing mental, emotional, physical, and spiritual information on each and every event. In this sense, you carry imprints of prior traumas, past triumphs, codependences, and everything else that goes into building up your experience in this life. This is true regardless of whether or not those experiences were positive or negative. Scarring, whether it be physical, emotional, or mental, is one manifestation of this phenomenon. When you hold onto old energy scars and traumas for an extended period of time, they have the potential to deteriorate your body, stop you from developing emotionally, and impede your spiritual connection as well as your pleasure in life. Because of this, the areas around your chakras will become overcrowded and unhealthy.

Susan Peck included a section in her 2017 report on the behavior of energy fields during death and near-death experiences in which she discussed her observations of the chakras shutting in order, beginning with the root chakra and working their way up to the crown chakra. She also described the patient's bodily condition after each closure, sharing how the patient's physical body shuts down as the chakras reach their final state. Despite the fact that contemporary medical research is unable to provide an explanation for why this is the case, the findings are sound and support what has been known about chakras from ancient times. (Peck, et al. 2017, to be exact)

While the regions of your body corresponding to your Root chakra all the way up to your Throat chakra vibrate and have an impact on the main nerve centers of your endocrine system, the higher two chakras do not. Both your Third Eye chakra and your Crown chakra are related to your pituitary gland and your pineal gland, which are located on your brainstem. These glands are associated with higher-level mental activities, feelings, and spirituality.

When all of this information is considered together, a more comprehensive picture emerges. The healing process is sped up and continuous life is made possible when chakras are in excellent condition. This benefits the areas of the body that the chakra dwells in, allowing them to recover from injuries more rapidly and to keep their health in good shape. Your chakras, tissues, muscles, and organs located in that region of your body, as well as you, are all experiencing joy right now.

Chakras and the State of One's Body

Your physical body and your health are powered by your lower chakras, namely your Root chakra, which is associated with your feet to hip regions and organs, and your Sacral chakra, which is associated with your lower belly. These chakras have an effect on your resistance to sickness as well as your physical strength and recuperation, as well as your digestion, sexual health, energy levels, and the amount of stress that your body experiences. In addition to this, they have an effect on your motor control and movement.

Chakras and one's mental and emotional health

Your mental health and the feelings associated with it are related to your middle chakras. Your Solar Plexus chakra is associated with your feeling of self-worth and your sense of identity, your Heart chakra is associated with your capacity to give and accept love, and your Throat chakra is associated with your ability to speak. The shifting energy of these chakras will have a direct effect on your states of mind. When these chakras are activated or grown, you will be forced to confront some tough and profound existential issues about yourself, love, and the experiences you have had with these things. They shed light on your ever-developing personality as well as your singularity.

Chakras and the State of Spiritual Health

You probably already have a good idea by now that the Third Eye and Crown chakras, which are your highest chakras, have something to do with your spiritual growth and development. They have a connection to your pineal gland as well as your pituitary gland. Your intuition, heightened senses (think of Spiderman's Spider sense), and increasing awareness are all taken care of by the Third Eye. Some people believe that your pineal gland is connected to your crown. You are able to have a knowledge of oneself that extends beyond your physical body as well as a deeper, more multidimensional comprehension of the cosmos and all that exists within it thanks to your Crown chakra. Many people believe that it is your link to your divine or higher self, which in certain cultures is referred to as your soul.

The opening of these two upper chakras paves the path for you to have a richer, more compassionate, and more relaxed experience of life.

The Chakra at the Crown

The seventh chakra center, similar to the sixth chakra center, links us to higher or alternative planes of existence; but, the connection established by the seventh chakra center is of a more varied and comprehensive kind. For the purpose of reaching complete enlightenment, the Crown chakra establishes a direct connection with either Source or our own Higher Selves. One way to think of the Higher Self is as an other version of oneself that understands everything about them, from the innermost parts of their existence to the things they present to the outside world. It comprehends you on a deeper level than you do yourself, and it really hopes that you find fulfillment in life and continue to grow as a person. Because you and the Higher Self are the same entity, this is the case. The only difference between the two of you is that you have your awareness anchored in the physical world, whilst the Higher Self exists on a somewhat higher level of existence (thus the term). Not only does this provide absolute insight, but it also grants you vast knowledge to apply that clarity effectively. The location of the Crown chakra is often shown as being at the very top of the head or floating slightly above it. Despite its name, the Crown chakra is associated with thought rather than any particular element. Its component is the act of thinking itself. Consider the implications of that for a while, all right?

With its emphasis on being One with all that has been created, the Saharara places a primary focus on universal connectivity as its major tenet. When one comes to this awareness, they are able to achieve inner peace and a general reduction in fear. It is essential to keep in mind that the knowledge gained here is not on an intellectual level, but rather a more general comprehension of the functions that are played by every living creature in the universe. The Crown chakra is the location where the exchange of cosmic energy and the life energy of an individual takes place, which strengthens one's connectedness to everyone. The Saharara, which acts as a natural type of receptor for energies that are freely flowing throughout the cosmos, takes in this energy and turns it into power, which enables us to transcend our physical boundaries. When we have reached the transcendent level, our awareness "pushes out" into the vastness of the cosmos, giving forth life energy to be accepted by everyone. This happens when we have become one with the universe. It is a cycle of flowing energy that maintains life, both physical and spiritual, across the whole of the known cosmos. This cycle can be found in every part of the universe.

The inability to maintain a healthy balance in the Third Eye chakra may result in a disconnection from the physical world and a preference for living purely in the mind. You start to feel an almost total disconnection from the material world, even your own body. It goes without saying that this has the potential to severely damage any relationships with other people. You could even find that you are unable to stick to any kind of objective or continuous plan of action at all throughout this time. It is possible to get severed from one's spiritual connection, leaving one firmly entrenched in the physical element. Headaches, migraines, nerve pain, sleeplessness, depression, and even potential schizophrenia are some of the physical symptoms that express themselves more often than others.

One would do well to meditate on a regular basis in order to ward against certain sorts of illness. Also, give some thought to the idea of a glorious white light penetrating the crown of your head and becoming a part of it. Regularly engaging in any of these activities will activate your Brow chakra, so enabling it to function in an optimal manner. As is usually the case, practicing a wide range of yoga positions may help enhance the overall health of your chakras, in addition to maintaining the strength of your body. The presence of the aromas of sandalwood or myrrh in a space that you want to reside in can assist in the removal of any leftover obstructions. One more piece of advice: since the sun's light is such a potent source of natural energy, spending some time letting your Saharara soak up some of its rays can help boost its health.

The Seven Chakras

As was said previously, your body is comprised of seven primary chakras, all of which are arranged in line with your spine. It is important to take notice that there are also some ancillary energy points. The energy moves from the crown of your head all the way down to the base of your spine thanks to the chakras. If the body is not in a state of balance, the impacts of each of these chakras, which are each symbolized by a different hue, will become apparent.

A chakra is tied to each of the colors in that each vibrates to a specific frequency and reacts to various wavelengths of light (color). This is how a chakra is connected to the colors. As a result, some information about one's physical, emotional, mental, or spiritual state is included within each hue. This information is used in the process of chakra healing and balancing, which is accomplished via the use of color healing.

The seven chakras are described as follows below:

1. The sahasrara, often known as the crown chakra

The color violet is said to be representative of this chakra. You may locate it at the very top of your head. There is a connection between it and the cerebral cortex, as well as the central nervous system and the pituitary gland. This chakra is associated with knowledge, joy, and the concepts of understanding and acceptance. The link between you and God is also supposed to be established via this chakra. Additionally, it determines both one's own fate and the heavenly purpose for their lives. A blockage of this chakra may lead to a number of imbalances, including photosensitivity, migraines, neuralgia, epilepsy, mental disease, skin rashes, and difficulties with right-brain coordination and abnormalities, as well as other psychological issues. This chakra may be activated through journaling one's ideas, innovations, and visions, as well as by concentrating intently on one's dreams.

2. The brow chakra, often known as the third eye.

The color indigo, which is created by combining blue and red, is said to be representative of this chakra. It will sit in the middle of your forehead, somewhat higher than or at the same height as your eyes. The third eye chakra is associated with psychic abilities and intuition. It opens the mind to new ideas, questions, and knowledge. This chakra stores your dreams for this life as well as those from previous lives. If this chakra is blocked, it may result in difficulties with learning, sleep disorders, sadness, a lack of foresight, and problems with coordination. These issues can also be caused by a lack of foresight. Stargazing and the observation of other indigo-colored items are two activities that might activate this chakra.

3. The visuddha, or throat, chakra

The area of your neck houses the fifth chakra, known as the throat chakra. This chakra is associated with the color turquoise or blue. This chakra is related to your neck, arms, shoulders, thyroid, hands, and parathyroid glands, and it is involved with communication, self-expression, creativity, and judgment. This chakra is responsible for both external and internal listening, as well as change, cleansing, and the synthesis of ideas. It is possible for this chakra to get blocked, which may result in swollen glands, thyroid imbalances, hyperactivity, influenza and fevers, infections, and hormonal abnormalities such as mood swings. The throat chakra may be activated by engaging in activities such as singing, poetry, painting, and stamp collecting; having meaningful discussions; and making use of things that are blue.

4. The anahata, or heart, chakra Thecolor green is associated with the anahata, or heart, chakra. It is rather evident that it is situated inside your heart. This chakra is where compassion, love, peace, and harmony are found at their core. The majority of Asians believe that it is where the soul resides. The thymus gland, the heart, the lungs, the arms, and the hands are all connected to the heart chakra. When we feel love for someone,

it is because of our heart chakra. Blocking this chakra may lead to problems with breathing and the heart, as well as breast and heart cancer, high blood pressure, chest discomfort, and even inhumanity, unprincipled conduct, or a lack of compassion. To clear this chakra's blockage, try going on walks in natural settings, spending time with your loved ones, and making use of things that are green or feature the color green, such as donning green clothes.

5. The chakra known as the solar plexus (manipura).

You may locate this chakra only a few inches above your navel, in the region of your solar plexus, and it has a golden tint. Your muscles, pancreas, adrenal glands, and digestive system are all involved in this condition. This chakra is where all of your feelings and emotions are stored and processed. This energy area is connected to the emotions of pleasure, laughter, power, and rage that you experience. Your capacity to succeed, your sensitivity, and your drive are all contained in this region. You may suffer from poor memory, digestive issues, ulcers, hypoglycemia, constipation, nervousness, diabetes, constipation, irritability, and frustration if this chakra is blocked.

Reading instructive books, enrolling in courses, engaging in mental puzzles, getting enough of sunlight, and taking part in detoxification programs are all excellent ways to keep the energy flowing effectively through this chakra. Utilizing things that are yellow in hue, such as wearing clothing that is yellow, is another way to assist in maintaining the flow of energy.

This chakra is represented as an orange hue and is located between your navel and your spine. It is also known as the sacral chakra, the navel chakra, and the spleen chakra. The kidneys, the lower abdomen, the bladder, the reproductive organs, the glands, and the circulatory system are all connected to this condition. It is involved with your feelings and emotions, which are represented by pleasure, desire, sexuality, creativity, and procreation. These are all important aspects of your life. A deficiency in the passage of energy to this chakra may result in concerns such as addiction to alcohol and drugs, eating disorders, depression, lower back pain, Candida and yeast infections, asthma and allergies, urinary problems, infertility, impotence, and sensuality issues. This may also show itself as sexual guilt, compulsive behavior, and several other emotional issues.

You may improve the flow of energy to this chakra by taking warm baths with essential oils, getting a massage, engaging in water aerobics, and making use of orange objects and practices, such as donning orange clothing.

7. The Muladhara Chakra, also known as the Root Chakra.

Your coccyx is the location of the root chakra, which is a fiery-red energy center at the very base of your spine. It is connected to your life and addresses issues with the physical and material world, as well as concerns of security and your capacity to advocate for yourself. An imbalance in this chakra may result in symptoms such as lethargy, anemia, sadness, soreness in the lower back, numbness in the feet and hands, and recurrent bouts of the common cold.

This chakra may be activated by getting enough rest, engaging in physical activity, creating art, or working in the garden. As is often the case, donning items of clothes that are red may also be of assistance in enhancing the energy flow inside your root chakra.

The third approach is to pray.

Just in case you were unaware, you pray each and every day. Yes, you! Whether you believe in gods or not, it makes no difference. You may be wondering, "But how?" You unconsciously start making this thing so big that it's your god now, and your daily thoughts towards this thing are prayer. Even if you are an atheist, you do believe in something because the human is programmed to believe in something. This something could be money or physics or even history or math. Simply relying on something for guidance and thinking that this thing will be the reason behind your happiness, success, and being in peace, and therefore, your daily thoughts are revolved around this thing as a large part of your day, is prayer. You don't have to get down on your knees or raise your hands in order to pray; all you need to do is think that this thing will be the reason behind your happiness, success, and being in peace.

Some individuals are under the impression that all they need to do to be considered believers is to read their Bible or Quran and visit their local mosque or church on a daily basis. If you want to know right now what you believe in, you should monitor your thoughts for a week and observe the topics that preoccupy your mind the most. It would be helpful if you could put in more effort and write things down in order to be more persistent. This would make the situation even better.

Let's move on to the power of prayer now that we've established what the term "prayer" refers to and established that what you believe in is what determines how you spend your day.

Researches have provided a lot of proof that prayer is highly strong. Starting with Andrew Newberg's brain scan, which reveals the difference between a believer in god's brain and a person who does not believe in god's brain as well as how prayer transforms the brain, researchers have proved that prayer is very powerful. The scan had showed that the nuns' brains, as well as Buddhist monks' brains, were more engaged during prayer. This was notably true of the lobes, and to be more precise, the orientation region. However, the nuns' brains were even more stimulated owing to the mixing between picturing and reciting during prayer.

Pray and make it perfectly clear to God and the world what it is that you want; then, ask to have your spirit and soul purified and cleaned. Through prayer, you are able to become one with God, and as a result, everything and everything is now within your reach. This is because prayer allows you to become one with the divine love, the divine light, and the divine grace.

Your life will change for the better if you pray consistently for ten minutes each day, but there are some guidelines to follow in order for your prayers to be answered:

The truth is that God, the cosmos knows you so well that it even knows you better than you know yourself. When you pray, be sincere; tell God what you truly want, and explain to him why you want it, as well as what will occur and improve as a result of its being manifested. However, by explaining to God why you want the thing you are requesting, as well as what will occur and improve as a result of its being manifested, you are only reminding yourself and giving yourself more clarity; you are not giving this information to God. BEING TRUE ENTITLES YOU TO RECEIVE ANYTHING FROM GOD.

- Always Remain Consistent: Inconsistency is where the magic occurs, because without it, nothing ever takes place. Is it possible to get a degree without really going to school or attending classes on a regular basis? Is it possible to love someone even if you do not spend a significant amount of time with them? You cannot get everything you want since there are rules and regulations in life that must be followed in order to achieve your goals.

- Pray aloud: the sound of your own voice has a great deal of influence on you. Did you know that you have a unique voiceprint just like you have a fingerprint? If you pray aloud and ask for what you desire while using your voice, your brain will get active, and you will experience a miraculous transformation.

This Is The Throat Chakra.

The color blue is said to symbolize the throat chakra, which is associated with speech as well as the expression of one's own personality. This chakra is in charge of regulating how intense our facial expressions are while we are interacting with other people and communicating with them. If you are able to open this chakra, you will have an easier time communicating with other people. You may look forward to improving your ability to communicate in an unrestricted manner.

People that have a healthy and open throat chakra exude an air of self-assurance. This quality endows them with likability and magnetism, and it is often the quality that enables them to distinguish themselves from the other individuals in the group. People whose neck chakras are open often express themselves creatively and have an interest in the visual arts or performing arts.

If the energy in this chakra is not flowing as it should, you may experience shyness and find it difficult, if not impossible, to speak out in large groups of people. People who suffer from stage fright often have issues related to a restricted throat chakra.

Your self-confidence will most likely suffer as a result of this, and you will find it tough to acknowledge when you have been unsuccessful and much more challenging to "start over." It is common for people who are going through such terrible times to withdraw within themselves and become more self-absorbed. Isolation and the utter lack of a social life are the only possible outcomes that can come from doing something like that. In addition to this, having a blocked throat chakra may lead to vices such as compulsive lying.

People whose throat chakra is overactive tend to be chatty to the point that it makes others around them uncomfortable. Their inflated sense of self-esteem gives them the appearance of being exceedingly haughty and superior. People who have this trait tend to speak more and listen less. They lack depth of thought and are often looked down upon by others around them. An overactive throat chakra not only makes you a poor listener, but it also functions as a huge barrier to learning new things and venturing into uncharted territory.

Because of this, opening the throat chakra may help you achieve a required balance in your expressiveness and social behaviour. This simple practice can assist you in opening your throat chakra so that you can take advantage of all of the advantages that come with doing so.

Repeat the position you have been practicing throughout the exercises in which you have been sitting on your knees. Allow your hands to hang at either side of your body in a relaxed and loose manner. Make an effort to get your body to loosen up and relax so you can feel better. Now, carefully lift your hands to shoulder height and interlace your fingers on the palms of both hands so that they form a cross. Be sure that your thumbs are pointing straight up and are touching one another. Once you have reached that posture, you should attempt to raise yourself up a little bit.

You should bring your hands up to your neck like this. Relax and make an effort to regain your calm by focusing on the throat chakra and all of the beneficial impacts it has on our body, in particular, as well as on life, in general. After you have achieved a state of relaxation, it is time to begin reciting the "HAM" mantra. When you are reciting the mantra, you should make sure that your mind is free of any thoughts about the outside world and that you are entirely concentrating on the function of the throat chakra.

If it is at all feasible, you should attempt to think on the positive impacts that this practice is having on your body while you are simultaneously releasing the negative effects of having a blocked throat chakra and having it opened. Maintain the same posture during the mantra practice, and do so until you can once again identify that sensation of cleanliness.

During this particular exercise, we strongly encourage our readers to maintain the steadiest possible control of both their hands and their heads. They will be better able to concentrate on the workout as well as the throat chakra itself as a result of this. The presence of your mind and your ability to exert control over your thoughts is the single most significant factor in determining the efficacy of your workouts, but even very straightforward advice like this may make a difference.

We hope that you are able to follow the recommendations and that you find it simple to incorporate them into your day-to-day activities. Let's move on to our last two chakras as fast as possible.

Symptoms Of A Disrupted Energy Balance In The Heart Chakra

If your Heart Chakra is out of balance, you may find it challenging to form partnerships that are both long-lasting and significant. Both having intimate relationships with other people and connecting with them on the most fundamental level will be challenging.

You could also be weak in empathy and compassion, which causes you to have a pessimistic outlook on life and perhaps feel hatred toward other people.

If you lack compassion, it will be difficult for you to comprehend the fact that other people have the freedom to make decisions with which you may not agree and that those decisions are theirs to make, not yours to make. In light of these facts, it is quite simple to lack compassion and slip into a judgemental mindset.

What Kinds of Health Problems Can Result from an Unbalanced Heart Chakra?

Because it often takes the form of a physical issue rather than a psychological one, this sort of imbalance is perhaps the most detrimental kind of imbalance that a person may have. Even breast cancer and heart illness have sometimes been connected to imbalances in the Heart Chakra; however, these are not diseases that can be remedied by drinking the appropriate colored drink or taking a warm bath.

Instabilities in this area may also create chest aches and difficulty in breathing, both of which are concerns that you would like to avoid having to deal with if at all possible. Even while no one completely comprehends the mechanism behind the potent impacts of the heart chakra, there is a great deal of evidence to show that this is the case.

Bringing Back the Sense of Balance to the Heart Chakra

When it comes to regaining a healthy balance in your heart chakra, the natural world is one of your most reliable partners. Spend as much time as possible walking in the woods or on the beach, spending as much time outside as you can when you can.

Also, prioritize quality time with the people you care about the most. This may help the Heart Chakra "remember" its duty and operate as it should more effectively. Spend the day catching up with your loved ones, but don't forget about your pals too. Spending time with the individuals who are important to you will help you maintain your equilibrium.

Green beverages and meals, as well as green essential oils, may all contribute to the recharging of the Heart Chakra.

This is the Throat Chakra.

It should come as no surprise that the throat houses this chakra since it is associated with speech and expression.

What exactly is the function of the Throat Chakra?

This chakra is responsible for regulating both your speech and your beliefs. Because of this energy, you are able to express your thoughts and worries, even if they run counter to what other people think and say.

Both your inner and your outside voices are given more force when you work with the Throat chakra.

Warning Signs That Your Throat Chakra Is Out of Balance

If the energy in your Throat Chakra is out of whack, you may find it challenging to communicate with others in a straightforward manner. When it comes time for you to articulate your ideas and viewpoints in front of other people, nervousness will get in the way and make it difficult for you to do so.

It's also possible that you'll start to mistrust other people, which, in turn, will make you less loyal to the ones who are essential to you. This vicious cycle may last a very long time.

Symptoms And Indications Of An Unbalanced Sacral Chakra

Experiencing low back discomfort, hip pain, or pelvic pain are all symptoms of an energetic imbalance in your Sacral Chakra. Additionally, it may entail difficulties with sexuality and reproduction, dysfunctions of the kidneys, and urine problems.

Concerns of betrayal and a lack of creative expression are all symptoms of an emotional imbalance, as are difficulties in expressing emotions, having fun, having obligations in your relationships, and having problems having fun. You may also be dealing with problems related to your sexuality and the pleasure you get from it, such as anxiety over impotence or addictions.

It's also possible that you're shy, that you struggle with trust and connection, that your emotions are all over the place, and that you're too sensitive. If your Sacral Chakra is not functioning properly, you may find that you are needy and that your behavior toward others is chilly and detached. Your fundamental emotional center is located in your sacral chakra, and virtually all of us, at some point in our lives, have struggled with an imbalance in this chakra.

How to Bring Your Sacral Chakra Back Into Balance

Your imagination will rise, you will be enthusiastic and extroverted, and you won't have any trouble taking chances when your Sacral Chakra is in harmony. You will have compassion, a grounded perspective, and an intuitive nature. You will have an open mind and be responsive to the things going on in the world. You will have a lot of energy, you will feel emotionally stable, you will be sexually stimulated, and you will have a lot of enthusiasm for life.

Now is the Time to Consider Orange

Imagine that your lower belly is being bathed in a soothing orange light that fills every available area. Send your breath together with the color orange to any part of your body that hurts, is tense, or is afflicted with a disease.

Don't You Want It?

Simply let go of all of those bad thoughts and memories, as well as the unhealthy individuals that have crossed your life, and turn them over to the cosmos. Instead of filling your space with unfavorable thoughts and feelings, it is much more vital for you to make room and energy for new and improved possibilities in your life. If you do not let go of this baggage, you will not have the room in your life necessary to make room for new vitality and prospects.

You will feel emotionally cut off from the world. Acquire the skill of trusting your own intuition, but do not give in to the temptation of letting your feelings control you. It is very normal for this not to come readily to you. It requires a lot of practice.

Time for yoga

Your hips are a storehouse for both the physical and mental strain that you carry. Because of this direct connection to the Sacral Chakra, yoga poses that focus on opening up the hips may be quite helpful to practitioners.

Are you still not persuaded? When you find yourself in a stressful situation, you should begin to become aware of the muscles that you tense up and clench. Your emotional centers are most likely located in the region of your neck, your lower belly, and your hips. These are the three most common locations.

Your hips may move in a number of different ways. Perform at least a couple positions in which you move your hips through their whole range of motion. Start by holding a single stance and concentrating on entirely letting go of your grip on the pose. The cow position (shown on the left) coupled with the cat pose (seen on the right) is a common combination.

Raise the Stakes!

It is essential that you take care of your body and engage in activities that will maintain your muscles healthy and powerful. Maintaining your muscle tone is an effective method for doing this, and doing so will also make it easier for you to break free of any clutching tendencies that are caused by your muscles.

Yoga not only gets your body ready for meditation but also turns it into a vessel for your soul to go through. It is an excellent instrument that may assist you in toning. A common problem region that has to be toned is the area of the lower abdominals. There are a number of great yoga postures that may help you tone the abdominal muscles, including the boat pose and the pendant pose.

The Chakra At The Crown

The seventh and last chakra, known as the crown chakra, may be found at the topmost pinnacle of one's head. Its energy is associated with the color violet. Because it is tied to our capacity to be totally connected spiritually and is associated with our level of self-awareness, the spirit may be said to be its element. Its gemstone is the pearl, and its counterpart in the solar system is the planet Pluto. Its emblem is a thousand-petaled lotus. The root chakra is symbolized by the spiral pair that it has.

The happiness of enlightened understanding is what stimulates a spirit of awareness and intellect in the crown chakra. When your crown chakra is clear, you are able to see the world and yourself without bias and with heightened awareness. People who are hooked to spirituality and egomaniacs are more likely to overlook their physical requirements and show signs of its extreme consequences, which may be seen in cult leaders. People who have an underactive crown chakra are oblivious of spirituality and have no feeling of spiritual ambition. This is because the crown chakra is located at the very top of the head. A crown chakra that is out of balance may cause ongoing irritation, emotions of destructiveness, and an inability to experience pleasure. If your crown chakra is healthy, you will have the power to connect with the divine and have unrestricted access to your subconscious mind. Migraines, despair, a lack of spiritual comfort, and difficulties with sleep and waking cycles are some of the conditions that are related with the crown chakra.

The crown chakra is symbolic of the greatest degree of awareness, enlightenment, and dynamic thinking. It is located at the very top of the head. It is the hub of connection to the spirit, and it integrates all of the chakras and the attributes they represent. Take note that this chakra is located outside of the body, is not connected to anything in the physical world, and has no connections other than those with pure awareness.

Meditation is the most effective method for restoring health to the top chakra.

Meditation For And Healing Of The Crown Chakra

Meditation is the greatest and most efficient approach to cure your crown chakra. This chakra is located at the top of your head. Because it kickstarts the process of these chakras being balanced, meditation is also a tried-and-true method for treating other chakras as well. Our day-to-day lives are centered on the specific ideas, feelings, and sensations that we encounter in our own reality; nevertheless, these specific notions hinder our capacity to advance to a level of awareness that is pure. The purpose of the practice of meditation is to release our minds from being obsessed with the details of daily life so that we may instead seek connection to a more profound dimension of our being.

Meditation is a practice that involves reprogramming our consciousness awareness, letting go of our connection to our current world, and progressing toward a state in which we are just aware of ourselves. Because of our awareness, we are able to tap into the force of pure consciousness and foster the conscious talents that would have otherwise remained dormant if we did not have this ability. The only way to really reap the advantages that meditation has to offer is to make it a daily habit and meditate for an extended period of time.

You will have a stronger fundamental connection to the bigger reality, which is the true source of all that you experience, if you engage in the practice of meditation regularly. You may try your hand at a variety of forms of meditation, such as mindful meditation, deep breathing, and so on. Find a method of meditation that is most effective for you, and stick with it.

When we make meditation a regular part of our lives, we cultivate the capacity to touch a level of pure awareness that is not only present during our individual meditation practices but also permeates every aspect of our lives. The practice of meditation instills one with a profound feeling of calm. The practice of meditation is equally significant since it helps us form a stronger connection with the spiritual wellspring of our life and wellbeing. Therefore, consistent practice ensures that we will develop a refined and improved body, mind, and spirit that is capable of performing at its absolute best, contributing a significant amount of serenity and harmony.

Acquiring A Wise Perspective

Wisdom is represented by the Agya chakra, which may be found in the middle of each of our heads. The destructive ideas and irrational beliefs that we hold onto are consumed by the energy that flows through this chakra. When spiritual energy begins to flow through the sixth chakra and start radiating outward, it guides us towards light and knowledge.

We are able to tell the difference between reality and our own interpretations of it. As we get closer to reaching a state of serenity, our intuitive skills get more refined, and they are better equipped to direct our thoughts and feelings.

We are aware that the challenges we faced in the past have had a role in shaping our mental and emotional condition at the present time. We are certain that we have moved on from the difficulties of the past and are pleased with the progress we have made in the present. But....

The reopening of old wounds may be triggered by anything as simple as a single event, a cutting phrase, or the sight of someone or something that is comparable to what we have experienced in the past. When we are confronted, tormented, and haunted by our previous failings, the delicate feeling of equilibrium that we had established for ourselves begins to disintegrate as a flood of competing emotions and thoughts begins to rage through us. However, despite the fact that our moral compass is robust and points us in the correct path, it seems that our emotions are winning the war. We are aware that we should not be thinking in this manner, but the passage of time has given us the impression that we are in a position of power, and this gives us the desire to exact revenge.

After that, we start looking for the companionship of that long-lost friend or cousin of ours, the one who has always believed in speaking the truth in a straightforward and straightforward manner. He maintained his impartiality and objectivity in his assessment of the situation, and he did what needed to be done in spite of the discomfort it caused him. He was a firm believer in fulfilling one's obligations to the best of one's abilities. He has arrived to the precarious condition of equanimity as a result of the experiences that he has had in his own life. And this is the mental and emotional condition that we, too, are longing to achieve.

A conversation with people of such ripe age bestows on us mental and moral lucidity as a result of the exchange. People who have progressed to such a spiritual level do not offer us advice or direct us toward a certain path. They provide us the ability to independently investigate and discover the truth. It is up to each of us to navigate our way out of the confusing web of contrasting feelings, ideas, and beliefs, as well as our own complicated histories.

They will bestow upon us the knowledge and insight that comes from their experience, which will enable us to live successful lives. They will not let the flow of spiritual energy to descend into the chakras below the agya chakra; rather, they will guide it upwards via the agya chakra in order to bring it higher.

Practices That Can Help You Out The sound "OM" is the mantra that corresponds with the Agya Chakra. The repetition of this mantra brings to a settling of our minds and a calming of our emotions. It contributes to the harmony of our mind, heart, and soul.

Reading enlightening literature and spending time with individuals who have developed their spirituality are two of the best ways to cleanse the Agya chakra. Our mental and emotional states have been refined. We grow better able to love and understand one another as well as create positive mental patterns.

Indigo is the color that is said to be connected with the Agya chakra. Crystals such as amethyst, ruby, unakite, and azurite are some examples of stones that may assist in the process of opening and balancing this chakra.

During our times of meditation, if we bring our attention to the concept of oneness, it will help us become in tune with the cosmos. Our knowledge leads us to believe that the whole of the cosmos is housed inside us in the form of this energy. This energy will direct us for the whole of our lives if we make the intentional effort to cultivate it.

Pranayama techniques such as KapalBhati and NadiShodhana are examples of breathing exercises that may be used to assist cleanse the agya chakra. The Akashi Mudra, as well as the many yoga mudras, the Bhumi pad mastak asana, the Shirshasana, and the Shashankasana are all examples of activities that are beneficial for this chakra.

The Chakra Of Love Located In The Heart

The fourth chakra, often known as the Heart Chakra, is situated in the middle of the chest. Its name comes from its location. It is a representation of love. An individual's development of the heart chakra typically starts between the ages of 22 and 28. The sense of touch, often known as the sense of feeling, is its sensory function. In addition to the cardiovascular system, the lungs, the rib cage, the skin, the arms, the hands, the upper back, and circulation are all connected to this chakra.

The color green is associated with the heart chakra. It is represented with a hexagon as its symbol. Air is the primary component of it. The letter "A" is spoken as part of its name. And this is consistent with the chant "YAM."

Acceptance may be bestowed onto others or received via the heart chakra, which functions as an internal channel. The force of love may be felt in this way, which provides the individual with both strength and comfort.

In addition to this, the fourth chakra acts as a conduit via which all of the other chakras may communicate with one another. The purpose of this chakra is to forge a connection that is in tune with both the individual's inner world and the wider cosmos. In contrast to the first four chakras, which place an emphasis on one's physical well-being, emotional experiences, and level of authority or power, the fifth chakra, the heart chakra, is concerned with matters that are external to oneself.

This chakra's function is to foster oneness among all forms of life and to draw that unity into one's own being. Only through providing and simultaneously receiving love, of an unconditional nature, is it possible to have a true sense of love.

Activating the Chakra of the Heart

Sit on the floor with your legs crossed and your back straight to open your heart chakra. Put the very tip of your index finger against the side of your thumb. After that, rest your left hand on your left knee using your left hand. Put your right hand in front of the breast bone, more especially in the lower half of the area, and hold it there. Put your attention on the heart chakra, which is positioned at the level of the heart on your spine. After then, you should begin repeating the word YAM.

The Value of Keeping Your Chakras in Check

A person's capacity for love may be gauged by how well their heart chakra is balanced. This person has a reputation for being kind and charitable toward others. It is more probable for people to have good relationships if the energy in their heart chakra is balanced.

These people have an approachable and friendly demeanor. They give off the impression of possessing a calm and collected demeanor. They make the intentional decision to love and to be happy, and as a result, their lives are filled with pleasure. They do not allow themselves to get preoccupied with events of the past, which enables them to move on.

What Occurs If There Is an Excessive Amount of Energy in the Heart Chakra

Those who have a heart chakra that is hyperactive often let their emotions get the best of them. Because of this, it is possible that they may exaggerate or overreact to the events that occur. They exist in the role of victims. They are believers in the concept of martyrdom.

Everyone experiences pain. On the other hand, if you have a heart chakra that is overdeveloped, you are more prone to experience suffering and brokenness in your life. It's possible that you won't be able to forgive. And the failure to forgive prevents the body from recovering. And if you haven't recovered from your wounds, you can't possibly go on with your life.

When your heart chakra is hyperactive, it might cause you to fixate on the past, which can cause you to ignore the here and now and cause you to forget about the future. As a result of this, you will most likely be able to discern the possibility of genuine partnerships.

You can be concerned about your safety because of the negative things that have happened to you in the past. You have an unhealthy fear of failing, which is why you do all in your power to steer clear of anything or anybody who may potentially do you harm.

A person's tendency for emotional outbursts may be a sign of an overworked heart chakra. Even though you may think of yourself as a hopeless romantic, if you don't restore the balance in this chakra, you will continue to have problems in your love relationships.

You run the risk of being too sensitive. Because of this, you could start to see conflicts as nothing more than assaults on your self. You could even get love and possessiveness mixed up in your head. It's also possible that you'll convince yourself — and feel justified in this belief — that you need the presence of another person in order to feel whole.

What Occurs When the Energy in the Heart Chakra Is Not Strong Enough

People who have a heart chakra that is not functioning properly often have social anxiety. They may be unable to forgive others or sympathize with those who have wronged them. Their lives may be characterized by a profound sense of isolation. These people have a tendency to have a cruel spirit and a narcissistic personality.

When the energy in a person's heart chakra is low, they may become emotionally distant. When the heart chakra is not healed and is out of balance, a person has a propensity to withdraw from other people and isolate themselves emotionally. It is possible for this individual to isolate themselves and maintain a mistrust of others.

Advice on Restoring Health and Restoring Balance to the Heart Chakra

In general, those who have an unbalanced heart chakra are more prone to have issues in their personal relationships. They could also have sensations of being cut off from others.

If your heart chakra is out of alignment, you may suffer from a variety of health concerns, such as asthma, skin disorders, heart illnesses and circulation conditions, as well as high or low blood pressure. You need to focus on your heart chakra for all of these reasons and more. The following recommendations should be of assistance to you in this endeavor.

Learn how to grant pardons.

You need to have the ability to forgive in order for this chakra to be healed. Consider making some changes. Find out what it is that you haven't completely let go of. Conduct a forthright analysis of the challenges you face.

Do you ever feel like a victim of someone or something else, even yourself? Then you need to ask yourself whether you can find it in your heart to let go of those difficulties, to stop playing the part of the victim, and to forgive your past as well as those who may have caused you grief and suffering in the past.

It is not something that can be accomplished easily. But you should give it a go.

Acquire an Attitude of Gratitude

This chakra encourages love that is not conditioned. And you may begin by focusing on yourself. The validation of practice. Put an end to your self-criticism and value who you are as a person, rather than focusing on the things you have accomplished or the possessions you have accumulated. When one first learns to appreciate himself, the subsequent step of learning to enjoy others might be a lot less difficult.

Practice meditation.

Try out this particular meditation technique to help repair your heart chakra.

Maintain an upright posture. Put your shoulders on your back and pull your chest upward so that it is exposed to the sky. Now, place the palm of your right hand on the center of your chest. It is recommended that the palm of your left hand be placed on the palm of your right hand.

Take a couple of slow, deep breaths in and out. Pay attention to the rhythm of your breathing. Observe how your chest expands and contracts with each breath you take. Close your eyes and see an item that is emerald green, whirling in your palm as it encircles your heart chakra. Feel your chest become warmer, more radiant, and entirely filled with the energy of love as it fills up completely. The energy should be poured into your heart chakra until it is completely saturated.

Keep going like this for the next five minutes. Bringing your attention back to your belly, take a few long, deep breaths, and then remove your hands from your chest to conclude this meditation practice. Finally, let the energy of love to become grounded in your chakra.

Make use of Crystal Therapy.

Make special use of the love stone or the rose quartz in this instance. It is said to have wonderful benefits on the chakra that controls the heart. This stone has the power to assist you in attracting all types of love, including love for your family, love for yourself, love for others, and romantic love.

You should start by reclining on your back. Find a position that's comfortable for you, and hold still. After that, position the rose quartz crystal such that it is directly in the centre of your chest. Take a number of calm, deep breaths in through your nose. While you're holding your breath, count to 10. Let the air out through your lips one slow breath at a time. Approximately 10 times should be spent going through this breathing practice. When you are finished, take the rose crystal out of its place and stand up.

Jade and aventurine are two more stones that work well with the heart chakra, in addition to rose quartz crystal. As an additional option, you may try using these crystals instead.

Aromatic oils like jasmine, rose, and tarragon may also be of assistance to you in the process of repairing your heart chakra. You are strongly advised to utilize herbs and spices like sage, basil, and thyme in your cooking. In addition, make it a point to include spinach, kale, and other leafy green vegetables into your diet on a regular basis since eating foods like these helps maintain a healthy heart chakra.

Obstacles Presented By The Chakras

Now that you are aware of what your chakras are, how they operate in your body, and the significance of them, it is a good idea to get an understanding of the "warning signs" that indicate when one or more of your chakras are out of balance. Your body will have a more difficult time functioning correctly as a result, which might lead to major health issues. However, something that you may have picked up on in the previous chapters is a reference to things like blocked chakras, hyperactive chakras, and underactive energy centers as well. Even the chakras in your body might exist in a "transitional" condition. The following is a quick tutorial that you may follow in order to determine what each of these phrases really means. It is a tool that may help you comprehend the changes that may occur in your energy while a certain chakra is functioning in a particular manner. This is just a guide, and you may experience your energy in a different way. When you sense that anything is "off," even though it does not seem to be the same as the descriptions in this chapter, trust your instincts and listen to them. As you become more connected with your True Self and the Universe, this will help you. Your body is intelligent, and it always attempts to achieve a state of equilibrium. If you can train yourself to pay attention to what it has to say and put your faith in what it asks of you, you will always be able to maintain a healthy level of energy.

Please refer to the following guidance in order to get an understanding of the numerous difficulties posed to the physical conditions of your chakras:

Having a chakra that is "open" indicates that it is doing its functions correctly. It is ready to take in and direct energy as it travels through your body to the appropriate destination. This is considered to be a "healthy" state.

A chakra that is not open to receiving new energy or sending out old energy is said to be "closed," and the most typical symptom of a closed chakra is avoidance. You could discover that you avoid engaging in particular activities or thinking specific ideas that are associated with the chakra that is blocked. If the chakra is closed, as opposed to just being blocked, this indicates that you have made conscious efforts to prevent this kind of energy from entering your energetic body. Because the energy associated with the impacted chakra has the potential to make you feel anxious or doubtful, you make an effort to prevent it from having any effect on you. When you suffer a physical injury or illness, it has the potential to shut a specific chakra linked with that body part. It's also possible for a chakra to become blocked due to unresolved emotional anguish from the past.

A "blocked" chakra is a chakra that is similar to a closed chakra, although there are some fundamental distinctions between the two. This word suggests that energy may still be able to flow in and out of a system, but that it is being impeded in some way. There is some kind of impediment in the way, which is making it difficult for the energy to flow. Your chakra will have difficulty becoming its completely expressed self as a result. Sometimes this is associated with a medical condition, while other times it is associated with an emotional one. Negative emotions or ideas may obstruct the passage of energy to a specific energy center. This can happen even when the energy center is not actively being used. There are instances when a person is "sort of" open, which means that they are open via their Root and Crown chakras, but there is a block on one or more of the interior five chakras. This may happen for a number of reasons. This indicates that the obstruction is not particularly serious; yet, it should still be dealt with in order to assist in better balancing the chakras and to give assistance to keep the Root and Crown chakras open. These seemingly insignificant roadblocks are often the result of internalizing the opinions of others towards your True Self.

On the other hand, the remainder of your chakras will become blocked if you have a closed Root chakra, Crown chakra, or all of these chakras. Because these two chakras are responsible for transporting energy from the universe into your body, this is why they are so important. Imagine that two rivers, one running in one way and entering the body from the crown of your head, and another flowing in the other direction and entering the body from the root chakra. These rivers are formed of energy, and they flow through your body, following the core channel that runs down the length of your spinal column. If either the Root or the Crown chakra is blocked, this river cannot flow, depriving the other chakras of their source of incoming energy. When this happens, it is vital to open the closed Root chakra and/or the Crown chakra before attempting to treat the other chakras that are blocked.

A chakra that is open yet acting with more zeal than is required might be said to be "overactive." It is conceivable for a chakra to be open while at the same time operating with more passion than is required. There is an excessive amount of focus and energy being directed onto this place and this aspect of your life. You may anticipate that the energy in the other chakras will be stressed or depleted when this occurs. When an excessive amount of energy is flowing through one chakra center for an extended period of time, it is possible that you may develop a sickness that is associated with this region. This ailment or disease is the result of overwhelming energy finally finding a way to express itself after having no other outlets available to it.

One that is "underactive" in the chakra system is sometimes referred to as a "blocked" chakra. This indicates that it is not receiving the necessary amount of energy for it to perform correctly, and as a result, it is failing. It is often impeded by an external force, which requires you to take action in order to restore equilibrium. For more information, please refer to the explanation given for the term "blocked" chakra.

An energetic "transitional state" for your chakras - There is no simple on-off button for your chakras to operate as there is for a light. It takes some time for them to get from one state to the next. The more effort you put into balancing them, the quicker and easier the shift will be, but it will not disappear. When you go from a closed state to an open state, as well as from an overactive or blocked state to an open one, you may anticipate changes in your being such as mood swings and other types of vacillations. Imagine a pendulum that is swinging back and forth before coming to rest in the center. Sometimes, you experience the hyperactive qualities, and other times, you experience the blocked circumstances, with amazing glimpses of balance in the swing. Sometimes, you experience the blocked situations with wonderful glimpses of balance. When the energy of your chakra is in this condition, it is natural for you to feel balanced in one moment and out of whack in the next. If you continue to work on and maintain the chakra's balance, over time you will notice that there is a greater overall equilibrium with less oscillations. The more you learn about your true nature, the easier it will be for you to return to this state of harmony whenever it is needed.

Despite the fact that each chakra is distinct and has particular qualities, there are obstacles that each chakra presents to your well-being when it is not operating correctly. Depending on the current condition of the chakra, the obstacles may sometimes seem as though they are on different ends of the spectrum. For instance, if one of your chakras is blocked, underactive, or hyperactive, it may hinder you from doing a certain activity, while the same chakra in an overactive condition may prevent you from being able to cease performing the action you are performing. The objective is to achieve a state of equilibrium, harmony, and moderation in all aspects of your life, including your thoughts and deeds.

When one of your chakras is blocked, you may just experience bodily symptoms, but when another chakra is blocked, you may have symptoms that are more mental in nature. Both of these symptoms are possible manifestations of the condition. It is important to be aware of the typical characteristics and issues that are associated with each chakra. This will allow you to readily recognize a problem long before it develops into something that you are unable to treat on your own, such as a life-threatening sickness. Your body will start to attempt to compensate for the absence of adequate energy flow as soon as one of your chakras is allowed to remain out of balance. It will show up as sicknesses, it will bring on intense symptoms, and it may even lead other energy centers to overcompensate or undercompensate. After some time has passed, this subsequently causes problems in those chakras as well. It is essential to bear in mind that in order to repair an imbalance in one of your chakras after it has manifested itself in a physical form in your body, you will need to address both the energy center and the physical manifestation. It is necessary to restore equilibrium to the energy center in order to not only aid in the ongoing recovery of the afflicted area of the body but also to forestall the emergence of other illnesses in the future.

www.ingramcontent.com/pod-product-compliance
Lightning Source LLC
Chambersburg PA
CBHW050413120526
44590CB00015B/1950